Learn all the key facts with CGP!

Want to remember all the crucial facts for AQA GCSE Computer Science?
This CGP Knowledge Organiser is here to help!

We've condensed every topic down to the vital definitions,
facts and diagrams, making it all easy to memorise.

To check you've really got your facts straight, there's also a matching
Knowledge Retriever book that'll test you on every page.

CGP — still the best! ☺

Our sole aim here at CGP is to produce the highest quality books —
carefully written, immaculately presented and dangerously close to being funny.

Then we work our socks off to get them out to you
— at the cheapest possible prices.

Contents

Section Six — Networks

Section Seven — Issues

Published by CGP.
Based on the classic CGP style created by Richard Parsons.

Editors: Martha Bozic, Liam Dyer, Sammy El-Bahrawy.

Contributor: Shaun Whorton

With thanks to Glenn Rogers and Shaun Whorton for the proofreading.
With thanks to Hannah Wilkie for the copyright research.

ISBN: 978 1 83774 133 5

Printed by Elanders Ltd, Newcastle upon Tyne.
Clipart from Corel®

Computational Thinking & Pseudo-code

Three Key Techniques for Computational Thinking

 ① **DECOMPOSITION** — breaking down a complex problem into lots of smaller ones.

 ② **ABSTRACTION** — simplifying a problem by picking out the important bits of information.

 ③ **ALGORITHMIC THINKING** — coming up with a series of logical steps to get from a problem to a solution.

Now for step 2...

EXAMPLE

Find the quickest route by car between two places.

① Decomposition: What is the length of each route?
What are the speed limits on each route?

② Abstraction:

Details to ignore	Details to focus on
Distance as the crow flies	Shortest route along the roads
Road names	Traffic information

③ Algorithmic thinking:
1) List all potential routes.
2) Find lengths of each route.
3) Calculate time for each route.
4) Find route with shortest time.

Pseudo-code

ALGORITHM — a set of instructions for solving a problem.

PSEUDO-CODE — a simple way of writing an algorithm without using a specific programming language.

There are no exact rules, but good pseudo-code will be:
• readable and easy to interpret
• not too vague
• structured like a piece of code
• easy to convert into any language

This book uses AQA pseudo-code.

EXAMPLE

Design an algorithm to filter items on a website so only those that cost £10 or less are shown.

```
n ← number of items
                        Loop goes
                        through each
FOR i ← 1 TO n          item one by one.
    itemPrice ← cost of item i
    IF itemPrice ≤ £10 THEN
        show item i
    ELSE
        hide item i     Checks whether
    ENDIF               each item should
ENDFOR                  be shown.
```

Flowcharts

Flowchart Symbols

Symbol	When It's Used
Start / Stop	At the beginning and end of the algorithm
Inputs/Outputs	For values that are put in or taken out
Processes	E.g. for instructions and calculations

Symbol	When It's Used
Decision	For a question — often a 'yes or no'
Subroutine	To reference other flowcharts
→	To connect boxes and show direction

Sequence

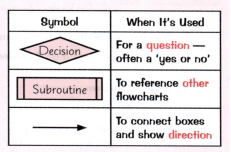

SEQUENCE — only has one route from start to stop.

A flowchart to find the cost of a hotel stay at £40 per night.

Start → INPUT number of nights → cost ← nights * £40 → OUTPUT cost → Stop

Selection

SELECTION — has decisions which give multiple routes from start to stop.

A flowchart to check a user is older than 12 before allowing access.

Start → INPUT age → Is age more than 12? — No → Deny access → Stop

Is age more than 12? — Yes → Allow access → Stop

Just go with the flow, man.

Iteration

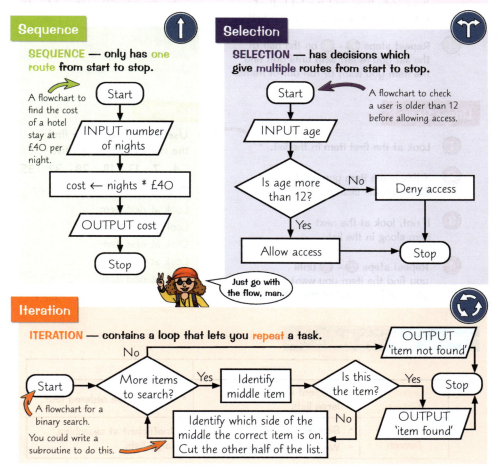

ITERATION — contains a loop that lets you repeat a task.

A flowchart for a binary search.

You could write a subroutine to do this.

Start → More items to search? — No → OUTPUT 'item not found' → Stop

More items to search? — Yes → Identify middle item → Is this the item? — Yes → OUTPUT 'item found' → Stop

Is this the item? — No → Identify which side of the middle the correct item is on. Cut the other half of the list.

Section One — Algorithms

Search Algorithms

Binary Search

The list must be ordered.

1. Find the middle item — for n items, do $\frac{(n+1)}{2}$ and round up if needed.

2. If this is the item you want, then stop the search.

3. If not, compare the two items. If the item you want comes after the middle item, cut the 1st half of the list. Otherwise cut the 2nd half.

4. Repeat steps 1 - 3 on the half of the list you're left with until you find the item you want or run out of items.

EXAMPLE

Use a binary search to find the number 32 in this list:

| 4 | 7 | 13 | 18 | 28 | 32 | 35 |

There are 7 items,
middle item is (7 + 1) ÷ 2 = 4th.
4th item is 18 and 18 < 32 so
cut first half of the list.

| 4̶ | 7̶ | 1̶3̶ | (18) | 28 | 32 | 35 |

There are 3 items left,
middle item is (3 + 1) ÷ 2 = 2nd.
2nd item is 32 so item found,
the search is complete.

Linear Search

1. Look at the first item in the list.

2. If this is the item you want, then stop the search.

3. If not, look at the next item along in the list.

4. Repeat steps 2 - 3 until you find the item you want or you reach the end of the list.

EXAMPLE

Use a linear search to find the number 32 in this list:

| 4 | 7 | 13 | 18 | 28 | 32 | 35 |

Check first item:	4 ≠ 32
Look at next item:	7 ≠ 32
Look at next item:	13 ≠ 32
Look at next item:	18 ≠ 32
Look at next item:	28 ≠ 32
Look at next item:	32 = 32

Item found — search complete.

Comparing Search Algorithms

	PROS	CONS
Binary Search	• Efficient at searching large lists	• List must be ordered first
Linear Search	• Simple • Works on unordered lists	• Inefficient at searching large lists

Sorting Algorithms

Bubble Sort

1. Look at the first two items in the list.

2. If they're in the right order, leave them. Otherwise, swap them.

3. Move on to the next pair of items (2nd and 3rd) and repeat step 2.

4. Repeat step 3 up to the end of the list — this is one pass. The last item is sorted, so skip it in the next pass.

5. Repeat steps 1 - 4 until there are no swaps left in a pass.

EXAMPLE

Use a bubble sort to write these letters in alphabetical order: P E N

1st pass:			Compare P and E
P	E	N	— swap them.
E	P	N	Compare P and N — swap them.
E	N	P	End of first pass.
2nd pass:			Compare E and N
E	N	P	— leave them.
E	N	P	No swaps so the list is sorted.

Merge Sort

1. Split the list into two sub-lists — start the second sub-list at the middle item.

2. Repeat step 1 on each sub-list until all sub-lists only contain one item.

3. Merge pairs of sub-lists back together. Each time you merge two sub-lists, sort the items into the right order.

4. Repeat step 3 until you've merged all the sub-lists together.

EXAMPLE

Use a merge sort to order these numbers from largest to smallest.

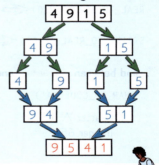

Comparing Sorting Algorithms

BUBBLE SORT	MERGE SORT
⊕ Simple and easy to implement	⊕ Efficient on large lists
⊕ Quick if list is already sorted	⊕ Running time unaffected by original order
⊕ Doesn't need much memory as sorting only uses original list	⊖ Goes through whole process even if list is already sorted
⊖ Inefficient on large lists	⊖ Uses more memory to create sub-lists

Data Types and Random Numbers

Five Basic Data Types

 INTEGER
- Whole numbers
- E.g. 0, –35, 1254

 REAL/FLOAT
- Decimal numbers
- E.g. 3.14, –150.2

 BOOLEAN
- Two values
- E.g. True/False, 1/0, yes/no

 CHARACTER
- One letter, digit or symbol
- E.g. 'X', '5', '?', '#'

5 STRING
- Text — a collection of characters
- E.g. 'Xm2Pe5', '@cgpbooks.co.uk'

Casting

Functions can convert between data types...

`STRING_TO_INT('5')` ⇐ String '5' to integer 5

`INT_TO_STRING(12)` ⇐ Integer 12 to string '12'

`REAL_TO_STRING(3.0)` ⇐ Real 3.0 to string '3.0'

`STRING_TO_REAL('2.0')` ⇐ String '2.0' to real 2.0

...and between characters and ASCII numbers.

`CHAR_TO_CODE('A')`

Character 'A' to integer 65

`CODE_TO_CHAR(65)`

Integer 65 to character 'A'

Choosing Data Types

Using correct data types makes code more:

1  Memory efficient

2 Robust

3 Predictable

Using the wrong data type could mean your code gives errors or unexpected results.

Random Number Generation

Generate random numbers by using this function. `RANDOM_INT(x, y)`

`RANDOM_INT(10, 99)` ⇐ A random integer between 10 and 99 (including 10 and 99).

`RANDOM_INT(-7, 0)` ⇐ A random integer between –7 and 0 (including –7 and 0).

Random numbers can be used to make unknown things happen in your program.
E.g. to make choices and set attributes randomly.

Level 82 Viking

–5 feet of fury

Operators

Arithmetic Operators

Perform maths functions on two integer or real values.

Operator	Function	Example	Result
+	Addition	4 + 5	9
−	Subtraction	6 - 9	-3
*	Multiplication	3 * 8	24
/	Division	35 / 5	7

Use these on integers only:

DIV	Integer Division	19 DIV 4	4
MOD	Remainder	19 MOD 4	3

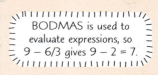

BODMAS is used to evaluate expressions, so $9 - 6/3$ gives $9 - 2 = 7$.

DIV gives the whole number part of a division.

MOD gives the remainder of a division.

Comparison Operators

Compare two expressions and return a Boolean value (True or False).

Operator	Meaning	Returns True	Returns False
=	is equal to	'A' = 'A'	'A' = 'B'
≠	is not equal to	6.5 ≠ 7.0	7 ≠ 7
<	is less than	8 < 9	6.5 < 6.5
>	is greater than	10 > 9	12 > 13
≤	is less than or equal to	6 ≤ 6	6 ≤ 5
≥	is greater than or equal to	1 ≥ 0	2 - 3 ≥ 0

Comparison operators are checked after other operators are performed.

Boolean Operators

Work with Boolean values/expressions and return True or False.

Operator	How it Works	Returns True	Returns False
NOT	Returns True when the expression is False.	NOT(6 < 5)	NOT(4 ≤ 5)
AND	Returns True when both expressions are True.	1 ≤ 1 AND 2 = 2	7 > 5 AND 1 < 0
OR	Returns True when either expression is True.	2 > 5 OR 3 < 6	4 ≥ 8 OR 6 = 9

Order of operations: brackets, NOT, AND then OR.

Variables and Strings

Storing Data Values

1. **Constants** can't change value while the code is running.

```
CONSTANT DAYSINWEEK ← 7
```

The **assignment operator** (←) assigns values.

2. **Variables** can change value.

```
length ← 3
length ← length * 10
```

- **Variable name (identifier)** on the left.
- **Value or expression** on the right.
- **Stored data values** can be accessed later in a program.

Make it descriptive.

Specify data types using a colon. ➡

```
age : Integer ← 16
```

Inputs and Outputs

Use **USERINPUT** to **get** data from a user.

```
name ← USERINPUT
```

Use **OUTPUT** to **display** data to a user.

```
OUTPUT 'An error occurred.'
```

Manipulating Strings

Strings can be written in single quotes.
Use the + operator to concatenate (join) strings.

```
str ← 'pear'
newStr ←'Ugh, my ' + str + ' is about to reap' + str
OUTPUT newStr
```

Function	Returns	Example	Result
LEN(string)	No. of characters	`LEN('Magic')`	5
POSITION(string, character)	First occurrence of a character	`POSITION('Magic','g')`	2
SUBSTRING(x, y, string)	String from position x to y	`SUBSTRING(2, 4, 'Magic')`	gic

EXAMPLE

Reformat the string variable 'name' so that the first character is moved to the end.

Strings are indexed from 0:

```
0 1 2 3 4
M a g i c
```

c has index (position) 4.

```
first ← SUBSTRING(0, 0, name)
rest ← SUBSTRING(1, LEN(name) - 1, name)
name ← rest + first
```

Extract the first letter.
Extract everything after.
Join the strings.

Selection

IF Statements

Check if a condition is True or False before running code.

IF statements start with 'IF [condition] THEN' and end with 'ENDIF'.

EXAMPLE

Code indented under 'THEN' ➡ is run when the condition is True.

```
IF tickets > 0 THEN
    OUTPUT 'Tickets available.'
ELSE
    OUTPUT 'Sorry, sold out!'
ENDIF
```

Code indented under 'ELSE' is run when the condition is False.

```
Start
Condition True?   Yes / No
Run code under 'THEN'
Run code under 'ELSE'
Stop
```

ELSE–IF Statements

Check different conditions and run the code under the first one that is True.

EXAMPLE

```
IF score > 90 THEN
    OUTPUT 'Amazing — well done!'
ELSE IF score > 60 THEN
    OUTPUT 'Great effort!'
ELSE IF score > 30 THEN
    OUTPUT 'Room for improvement!'
ELSE
    OUTPUT 'Keep practising!'
ENDIF
```

What to do if ...

...first condition is True.

...first condition is False, second condition is True.

...first and second conditions are False, third condition is True.

...all conditions are False.

CASE Statements

Check if a variable has specific values before running code.

The value of 'answer' determines which case to use.

Each case should be indented to the same place.

DEFAULT case comes at the end and is used if no other case is correct.

EXAMPLE

```
OUTPUT 'What is 5 - 7?'
answer ← USERINPUT
CASE answer OF
    -2:
        OUTPUT 'Correct!'
    2:
        OUTPUT 'Forgot minus sign?'
    DEFAULT:
        OUTPUT 'Wrong!'
ENDCASE
```

CASE only checks a single variable, not multiple conditions like ELSE–IF.

Iteration

FOR Loops

Repeat code a fixed number of times.

Set an initial value, end value and step count (optional).

```
FOR k ← 1 TO 9 STEP 2
    OUTPUT k
ENDFOR
```

Counts up in steps of 2.

Counter variable can be used inside loop.

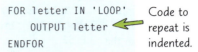
FOR loops are count-controlled.

Or use 'FOR-IN' for characters in a string or elements in an array.

```
FOR letter IN 'LOOP'
    OUTPUT letter
ENDFOR
```

Code to repeat is indented.

REPEAT-UNTIL Loops

Repeats until a condition is True. Condition checked at end of loop.

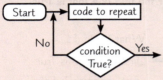

Always runs code at least once. Infinite loop if condition always False.

DO-WHILE Loops

Repeats while a condition is True. Condition checked at end of loop.

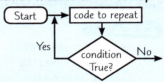

Always runs code at least once. Infinite loop if condition always True.

WHILE Loops

Repeats while a condition is True. Condition checked at start of loop.

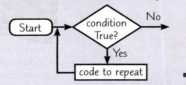

Never runs code if condition is False. Infinite loop if condition always True.

REPEAT-UNTIL, DO-WHILE and WHILE loops are condition-controlled.

LOOP-THE Loops

Repeat until queasy.

EXAMPLE

Write code for a darts game that counts down from 301. Stop when the player reaches 0. If they go under 0, ask them to throw again.

```
target ← 301
WHILE target ≠ 0
    throw ← USERINPUT
    IF target - throw < 0 THEN
        OUTPUT 'Throw again'
    ELSE
        target ← target - throw
    ENDIF
    OUTPUT target
ENDWHILE
```

For REPEAT-UNTIL or DO-WHILE, check 'target' at the end of the loop.

Checking Multiple Conditions

Nested Selection Statements

Make another selection depending on the outcome of a previous selection.

EXAMPLE

Write an algorithm that checks a user's age. If they're under 9, ask them to multiply their age by 7 and check their answer. Print a different message for each possible outcome.

Indentation makes nested statements more readable.

There can be statements nested inside the 'IF' part, the 'ELSE' part, or both.

```
OUTPUT 'What is your age?'
age ← USERINPUT
IF age < 9 THEN
    OUTPUT 'Multiply your age by 7.'
    answer ← USERINPUT
    IF answer = age * 7 THEN
        OUTPUT 'That's correct!'
    ELSE
        OUTPUT 'Learn the 7 times table.'
    ENDIF
ELSE
    OUTPUT 'You're too old for this test.'
ENDIF
```

Using Boolean Operators

Come on Meg, think. What was it?

Boolean operators can be used in selection and iteration statements to check more than one condition at once.

EXAMPLE

Use a WHILE loop to give 3 attempts to enter one of two valid passwords ('Meg123' or 'Adm1n!'). Once a valid password is entered, set 'access' to True and exit the loop, otherwise 'access' should be False.

```
attempts ← 0
access ← False
WHILE attempts < 3 AND access = False
    OUTPUT 'Password:'
    pw ← USERINPUT
    attempts ← attempts + 1
    IF pw = 'Meg123' OR pw = 'Adm1n!' THEN
        access ← True
    ENDIF
ENDWHILE
```

Repeat while fewer than 3 attempts have been made, and while access is False.

Check both passwords in a single IF statement condition.

Arrays

Purpose of Arrays

ARRAY — a data structure that stores a collection of values with the same data type.

- Each value is called an element.
- Elements are accessed by position (index), starting at position 0.

One-Dimensional Arrays

A 1D array is like a list.

You can create an array with square brackets and assigning values.

```
friends ← ['Abi', 'Ben', 'Cho']
```
3 elements (at positions 0, 1 and 2).

Retrieve elements by position.

```
OUTPUT friends[0]
```

```
Abi
```

Change elements by assigning new values.

```
friends[1] ← 'Bilal'
```

Replaces element at position 1 ('Ben') with 'Bilal'.

Find length (number of elements) with LEN.

```
LEN(friends)
```
3

Super
secret
int-el

Two-Dimensional Arrays

A 2D array is like a table. You can also think of them
as a 1D array where each element is a 1D array.

Positions of elements are written like [a][b] or [a, b].

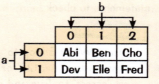

	0	1	2
0	Abi	Ben	Cho
1	Dev	Elle	Fred

EXAMPLE

The 2D array 'runs' is used to store the number of runs scored by two
cricketers in their last four matches. E.g. runs[2][0] returns 65.

Write an algorithm to set all values in the array back to 0.

The i FOR loop goes
through the 4 rows.

The j FOR loop goes
through the 2 columns.

```
FOR i ← 0 to 3
    FOR j ← 0 to 1
        runs[i][j] ← 0
    ENDFOR
ENDFOR
```

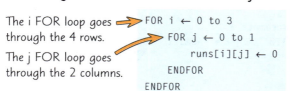

		Cricketer	
		0	1
Match	0	54	14
	1	83	22
	2	65	37
	3	58	26

Records

Purpose of Records

RECORD — a data structure that stores related values of different data types.
- Each element of a record is called a **field**.
- Records are **fixed** — more fields can't be added once created.

Creating Records

Create a record structure by giving a data type and name for each field.

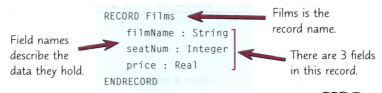

```
RECORD Films
    filmName : String
    seatNum : Integer
    price : Real
ENDRECORD
```

Field names describe the data they hold.

Films is the record name.

There are 3 fields in this record.

Create a record by assigning a variable with the same record structure:

```
ticket1 ← Films('Data Force', 16, 7.99)
```

filmName   seatNum   price

Use the variable name to access a whole record...

```
OUTPUT ticket1
```

```
('Data Force', 16, 7.99)
```

...and the field name to access or change values of a single field.

```
OUTPUT ticket1.seatNum
```

```
16
```

Grouping Records

You can group records with the same structure into an array.

	filmName	seatNum	price
0	Data Force	16	7.99
1	Record Ralph	10	6.00
2	The Constant	28	7.50

```
allTickets ← [ticket1, ticket2, ticket3]
FOR i ← 0 TO 2
    allTickets[i].price ← 5.00
ENDFOR
```

Changes the price of each ticket to 5.00.

Subroutines

Key Definitions

SUBROUTINE	A set of instructions stored under one name that are executed when called. They help to improve code structure, improve readability and avoid repeating code.
PARAMETER	A variable used to pass data into a subroutine. Can be any data type (e.g. integer, string, array, etc.).
LOCAL VARIABLE	Can only be used within the structure they're declared in.
GLOBAL VARIABLE	Declared with the keyword 'global'. Can be used any time after declaration, in any part of the program.

Procedures

PROCEDURE — a subroutine that doesn't return a value.

Subroutines are declared with a name and parameters in brackets.

Call a subroutine using its name. Pass data in using brackets.

EXAMPLE

```
SUBROUTINE outputSquare(number)
    OUTPUT (number * number)
ENDSUBROUTINE
outputSquare(5)
```
25

Functions

FUNCTION — a subroutine that does return a value.

EXAMPLE

Write a subroutine to reverse a string. Show it working on the string '!olleH'.

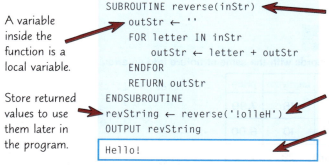

A variable inside the function is a local variable.

Store returned values to use them later in the program.

```
SUBROUTINE reverse(inStr)
    outStr ← ''
    FOR letter IN inStr
        outStr ← letter + outStr
    ENDFOR
    RETURN outStr
ENDSUBROUTINE
revString ← reverse('!olleH')
OUTPUT revString
```
Hello!

reverse is the function name and inStr is the parameter.

'!olleH' is passed into the function.

'Hello!' is the returned value.

Python

Data Types

Create variables using the **= operator**.
Data types are assigned automatically.

Whole number	Integer
Decimal number	Float
"Stuff in quotation marks"	String
True/False	Boolean

Casting functions change data types:

`str()` ⟹ convert to string

`int()` ⟹ convert to integer
(works on string or float)

`float()` ⟹ convert to float
(works on string or integer)

Operators

Use these operators as normal. `+  -  *  /`   `<  >`

//	Integer division
%	Remainder

==	is equal to
!=	is not equal to
<=	is less than or equal to
>=	is greater than or equal to

Boolean operators (and, or, not) in Python are in **lower case**.

Inputs and Outputs

Use **input()** to **get** data from a user.

Use **print()** to **display** data to a user.

```
name = input("Name my pet ferret. ")
print(name, "huh? I was thinking Zeus.")
```

Use commas to print multiple things — this separates values with spaces.

Prompt the user with a string inside the brackets.

Manipulating Strings

Use single or double quotes for Python strings — just be consistent.
Concatenate with the **+ operator**.

Use **casting** to combine strings with other data types. ⟹

```
stock = 15
message = str(stock) + " books in stock."
```

Function/Method	Returns
len(string)	No. of characters
string.find(substring)	First occurrence of substring
string[x]	Character at position x
string[x:y]	Substring from position x to before position y

```
genre = "fantasy"
print(genre.find("ant"))
print(genre[0])
print(genre[3:6])
```

```
1
f
tas
```

Strings (and data structures) in Python are indexed from O.

More Python

Selection and Iteration

Two important things to do:
- **Indent** to show where a statement starts & ends.
- Use a **colon** before an indented block of code.

Python statements

Selection: **if, if-else, if-elif**

Iteration: **while, for** loops

EXAMPLE

Write code to output the first 5 square numbers.

Code 'inside' the loop is indented.

```
x = 1
while x <= 5:
    print(x * x)
    x = x + 1
```

Super important colon.

range (x, y) counts up from x and stops just before y.

```
for x in range(1, 6):
    print(x * x)
```

Data Structures

LIST — Python data structure. Like an array, but can store different data types.

```
up = [1, 2, 3, 99]
up[2] = "missafew"
up.append(100)
```

Replaces item in position 2.

append() adds an item to end of a list.

```
print(up)
```

```
[1, 2, missafew, 99, 100]
```

Use **classes** to create **record structures**.

Set parameters (include **self**) and fields:

```
class Party:
    def __init__(self, nm, iv):
        self.name = nm
        self.invited = iv
```

Constructor subroutine.

Fields →

Create a record using the class name:

```
guest1 = Party("Omar", True)
```

Subroutines

1 Start with the keyword 'def'.

2 Give the subroutine a name.

3 Define your parameters.

4 Return values using 'return'.

optional

EXAMPLE

Write a subroutine that returns True if a given number is divisible by 3.

```
def divthree(number):
    if number % 3 == 0:
        return True
    else:
        return False
```

number is a local variable.

Modules

External Python files that often contain functions.

Use '**import**', then call functions with '**module.function**'.

```
import random
x = random.randrange(0,10)
```

Generates an integer from 0 to 9.

Structured Programming

Using Structured Programming

1. Decompose the program into manageable modules.

2. Continue decomposing modules into smaller modules, until each one performs a simple task.

3. Write subroutines to carry out each task.

4. Build the bigger modules and main program from the subroutines.

The interface of each module can be shown in a table listing its inputs, processes and return values.

You look a little decomposed...

You think?

EXAMPLE

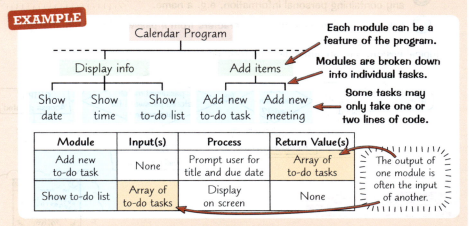

Calendar Program

Display info

Add items

Show date | Show time | Show to-do list | Add new to-do task | Add new meeting

Each module can be a feature of the program.

Modules are broken down into individual tasks.

Some tasks may only take one or two lines of code.

Module	Input(s)	Process	Return Value(s)
Add new to-do task	None	Prompt user for title and due date	Array of to-do tasks
Show to-do list	Array of to-do tasks	Display on screen	None

The output of one module is often the input of another.

The advantage of using structured programming is that modules can be...

 Written independently Tested individually Reused elsewhere

Four Ways to Improve Maintainability

Well-maintained code is easier for other programmers to understand. They can change parts of the code without causing problems elsewhere.

1. Write comments to explain what code does.

  2. Use indentation to make program flow clear to see.

Comments are usually written after # or //.

3. Use descriptive names for variables, subroutines and parameters so it's easier to keep track of them.

4. Only use global variables when necessary.

STRING whereTo
INT howFar

Authentication and Validation

Authentication

AUTHENTICATION — confirming the identity of a user before allowing access. Passwords or biometrics are usually associated with a username.

Four ways to make passwords more secure:

1 Force strong passwords — long with a mix of letters, numbers and symbols.

2 Limit the number of failed authentication attempts.

3 Refuse generic passwords, e.g. 'password123', and any containing personal information, e.g. a name.

Too much authentication can make a program less convenient for the user.

4 Ask for a random selection of characters from a password on each attempt.

Typical structure of an authentication routine:

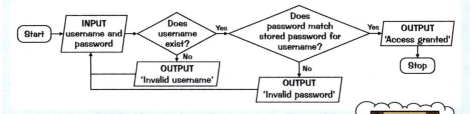

Five Validation Checks

INPUT VALIDATION — checking if data meets certain criteria before passing it into a program.

Programs often use a mixture of validation checks, including:

Anne's presence check wasn't very conclusive.

Validation check	What it does	Example code
1 Range check	Checks the data is within a specified range.	`IF age > 0` `AND age < 125 THEN`
2 Presence check	Checks the data has actually been entered.	`IF LEN(input) ≠ 0 THEN`
3 Format check	Checks the data has the correct format, e.g. a date.	`IF SUBSTRING(2,2,date)` `= '/' THEN`
4 Look-up table	Checks the data against a table of acceptable values.	`FOR val IN myList` `    IF input = val THEN`
5 Length check	Checks the data is the correct length.	`IF LEN(pin) = 4 THEN`

Testing

Two Types of Error

1 **SYNTAX ERROR** — when the rules or grammar of the programming language have been broken.

2 **LOGIC ERROR** — when a program is able to run, but does something unexpected.

Syntax errors are usually easier to spot since they will stop the program from running.

EXAMPLE

This function should check if a number is in a range.

Identify the syntax and logic errors.

```
SUBROUTINE inRange(n, min, max
    IF n > min OR n < max THEN
        RETURN True
    ELSE
        RETURN False
    ENDIF
ENDSUBROUTINE
```

Syntax error: In line 1, there is a closing bracket missing at the end of the line.

Logic error: In line 2, the 'OR' operator won't always lead to the desired outcome — both conditions need to be true to get the correct result, so the 'AND' operator should be used there instead.

Three Types of Test Data

TEST PLAN — a detailed plan of how a program is going to be tested, including what test data will be used.

TEST DATA — inputs chosen to see if a program is working properly.

1 **NORMAL DATA** — valid data that users are likely to enter.

2 **BOUNDARY DATA** — valid or invalid data at the limit of what should be accepted.

3 **ERRONEOUS DATA** — invalid data that should be rejected.

EXAMPLE

This heat should be rejected...

Complete this test plan for setting a digital thermostat. It should accept temperatures in the range 5-30 °C.

Type	Test data	Reason for testing	Expected outcome
Normal	12	Check normal usage.	Temperature accepted
Boundary	30	Check the largest value.	Temperature accepted
Boundary	31	Check too large values are rejected.	Error: too large.
Erroneous	'X'	Check non-numeric data.	Error: not recognised.

Trace Tables and Time Efficiency

Trace Tables

Trace tables keep track of the value certain **variables** take as a program runs.

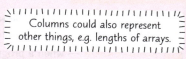

Columns could also represent other things, e.g. lengths of arrays.

- Columns usually represent variables.
- Rows show values of variables at a particular point.

They can be used to check for logic errors or to work out what a program is doing.

EXAMPLE

Complete the trace table when the algorithm below is run.
Explain what the algorithm does.

```
a ← 2
b ← 3
c ← 0
FOR i ← 1 TO b
    c ← c + a
ENDFOR
OUTPUT c
```

i	a	b	c
—	2	3	0
1	2	3	2
2	2	3	4
3	2	3	6

← Each variable has a column.
← Values before the FOR loop.
← a is added to c each time i increases.
← Last value of c is output.

The algorithm calculates a × b and outputs the result.

Time Efficiency

TIME EFFICIENCY — the 'time' it takes for an algorithm to complete a task, often in terms of things like number of **CPU cycles**, or how many times memory is accessed.

Things that can reduce time efficiency include:

 Having extra lines of code

 Using unnecessary loops

EXAMPLE

Compare the efficiency of these algorithms, and the one in the example above.

All three of these algorithms produce exactly the same result.

```
a ← 2
b ← 3
c ← a * b
OUTPUT c
```

This algorithm removes the FOR loop, so is more efficient than the one above.

```
a ← 2
b ← 3
OUTPUT a * b
```

This one avoids declaring a third variable, so is the most efficient of the three algorithms.

Number Systems

Three Important Number Systems

1 DECIMAL (BASE 10)
- Ten digits: 0, 1, 2, 3, 4, 5, 6, 7, 8 and 9
- Place values are powers of 10 (100s, 10s, 1s).

2 BINARY (BASE 2)
- Two digits: 0 and 1
- Place values are powers of 2 (8s, 4s, 2s, 1s).

3 HEXADECIMAL (BASE 16)
- Sixteen digits: 0, 1, 2, 3, 4, 5, 6, 7, 8, 9, A, B, C, D, E and F
- Place values are powers of 16 (256s, 16s, 1s).

Programmers like hex because the numbers are short and easy to remember, and can be easily converted to binary.

Decimal	Binary	Hex
0	0000	0
1	0001	1
2	0010	2
3	0011	3
4	0100	4
5	0101	5

Decimal	Binary	Hex
6	0110	6
7	0111	7
8	1000	8
9	1001	9
10	1010	A

Decimal	Binary	Hex
11	1011	B
12	1100	C
13	1101	D
14	1110	E
15	1111	F

Converting Binary to Decimal...

1 Put the number in a binary place value table.

2 Add up the place values in columns where there's a 1.

EXAMPLE

Convert 10011100 from binary to decimal.

1

128	64	32	16	8	4	2	1
1	0	0	1	1	1	0	0

2 $128 + 16 + 8 + 4 = 156$

...and Decimal to Binary

1 Draw a binary place value table.

2 Keep subtracting the biggest place values you can until you're left with 0.

3 If you subtracted a place value, put a 1 in that column, otherwise put a 0.

EXAMPLE

Convert 170 from decimal to binary.

1

128	64	32	16	8	4	2	1

2 $170 - 128 = 42$ $10 - 8 = 2$
   $42 - 32 = 10$ $2 - 2 = 0$

3

128	64	32	16	8	4	2	1
1	0	1	0	1	0	1	0

Converting Hexadecimal

Converting Hex to Decimal...

1. Put the number in a hex place value table.

2. Multiply (in decimal) the values in each column.

3. Add up the results.

EXAMPLE

Convert A2 from hexadecimal to decimal.

1.

16	1
A	2

2. A in hex is 10 in decimal, so: $10 \times 16 = 160$

$2 \times 1 = 2$

3. A2 is $160 + 2 = 162$ in decimal.

...and Decimal to Hex

1. Divide by 16 to get a quotient and a remainder.

2. Convert each value to hex.

3. The quotient is the 1st digit and the remainder is the 2nd.

EXAMPLE

Convert 43 from decimal to hexadecimal.

1. $43 \div 16 = 2$ remainder 11

2. 2 in decimal is 2 in hex.   11 in decimal is B in hex.

3. 43 is 2B in hexadecimal.

Converting Binary to Hex...

1. Put the number in a table that repeats 8, 4, 2, 1, ... Add zeros to the front so that it splits into nibbles.

2. For each nibble, add up the place values in columns where there's a 1, and convert into hex.

EXAMPLE

Convert 110 1101 from binary to hex.

1.

8	4	2	1	8	4	2	1
0	1	1	0	1	1	0	1

2. $4 + 2 = 6$ $8 + 4 + 1 = 13$

6 in decimal is 6 in hex.   13 in decimal is D in hex.

So 110 1101 is 6D in hexadecimal.

...and Hex to Binary

1. Convert each hex digit into a 4-bit binary number.

2. Put the nibbles together.

EXAMPLE

Convert E4 from hexadecimal to binary.

1. E in hex is 14 in decimal, which is 1110 in binary.   4 in hex is 4 in decimal, which is 0100 in binary.

2. So E4 is 1110 0100 in binary.

Using Binary

Binary Addition

To add binary numbers, use column addition.

Remember the four simple rules:

① 0 + 0 = 0

② 0 + 1 = 1

③ 1 + 1 = 10 (carry a 1)

④ 1 + 1 + 1 = 11 (carry a 1)

Fill the gaps to the left of the shorter numbers with Os, so they all have the same number of bits.

EXAMPLE

Work out the sum of the binary numbers 1101010, 111001 and 10001.

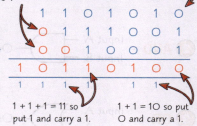

Add the columns from right to left.

Fill gaps with Os, so each number is 7 bits.

```
  1 1 O 1 O 1 O
  O 1 1 1 O O 1
+ O O 1 O O O 1
  ─────────────
  1 O 1 1 O 1 O O
  1 1 1 1   1 1
```

1 + 1 + 1 = 11 so put 1 and carry a 1.

1 + 1 = 1O so put O and carry a 1.

Binary Shifts

BINARY SHIFT — move every bit in a binary number left or right a certain number of places.

Gaps at the beginning or end of the number are filled in with Os.

Left shifts **MULTIPLY**. For every place shifted left, the number is doubled.

Right shifts **DIVIDE**. For every place shifted right, the number is halved.

A binary shift can result in an unexpected answer as bits can 'drop off' the ends and be lost.

- Losing 1s in a left shift gives a wrong answer to a multiplication.
- Losing 1s in a right shift gives an inaccurate answer (it rounds down).

EXAMPLE

Describe the effect of a 2-place left shift on O1O11101.

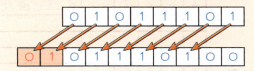

The number has been doubled twice, or multiplied by $2^2 = 4$.

If there are only 8 bits available to store the result, then a 1 will drop off the end and the answer will be wrong.

Boolean Logic

Four Types of Logic Gates

Logic gates receive binary data, apply a Boolean operation, then output a binary result.

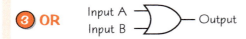

① NOT Input A ──▷∘── Output

NOT A
$\overline{A}$

Input A	Input B	Output
0	–	1
1	–	0

② AND Input A / Input B ──── Output

A AND B
A . B

0	0	0
0	1	0
1	0	0
1	1	1

③ OR Input A / Input B ──── Output

A OR B
A + B

0	0	0
0	1	1
1	0	1
1	1	1

④ XOR Input A / Input B ──── Output

A XOR B
$A \oplus B$

0	0	0
0	1	1
1	0	1
1	1	0

Combining Logic Gates

Logic gates can be combined into circuits.

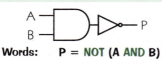

Words: P = NOT (A AND B)
Symbols: P = $\overline{A . B}$

Operations in brackets are done first.

A	B	A AND B	NOT (A AND B)
0	0	0	1
0	1	0	1
1	0	0	1
1	1	1	0

Two-Level Logic Circuits

Two-level means each input passes through at most two gates.

Words: Q = (NOT A) XOR (B AND C)
Symbols: Q = $\overline{A} \oplus (B . C)$

A	B	C	$\overline{A}$	B.C	Q = $\overline{A} \oplus (B . C)$
0	0	0	1	0	1
1	1	0	0	0	0
1	1	1	0	1	1

Full truth table has $2^3 = 8$ rows as there are 3 inputs.

Units and Compression

Seven Units of Data Size

Computers can only store and process binary data.

They use 1s and 0s to represent the flow of electricity — a 1 shows that electricity is flowing, and a 0 shows that it isn't flowing.

Each 1 or 0 in binary data is a bit (binary digit). The size of a file is the number of 1s and 0s that make up its data.

Traditionally, each unit is defined to be 1024 times bigger than the previous one.

Name	Size
① Bit (b)	A single binary digit (1 or 0)
② Nibble	4 bits
③ Byte (B)	8 bits
④ Kilobyte (kB)	1000 bytes
⑤ Megabyte (MB)	1000 kilobytes
⑥ Gigabyte (GB)	1000 megabytes
⑦ Terabyte (TB)	1000 gigabytes

Data Compression

DATA COMPRESSION — making file sizes smaller, while trying to stay as true to the original as possible.

Benefits of data compression:
- Compressed files use less storage space.
- Streaming/downloading compressed files takes less bandwidth.
- Some services like email have file size limits — compression can get a file below the limit.

Two Types of Compression

① **LOSSY COMPRESSION** — permanently removes data from the file.

② **LOSSLESS COMPRESSION** — temporarily removes data to store the file, and restores it to its original state when opened.

	Pros	Cons
Lossy	• Big reduction in file size, so they can be stored easier, and downloaded faster. • Commonly used — lots of software can read lossy files.	• Loses data — the file can't be turned back into the original. • Can't be used on text/software. • Reduction in quality.
Lossless	• No reduction in quality. • File can be turned back into the original. • Can be used on text/software.	• Comparatively small reduction in file size — lossless files take up more storage space than lossy files.

Characters

Character Sets

CHARACTERS — uppercase and lowercase letters, the digits 0-9, and symbols like ?, + and £. Used to make words and strings.

CHARACTER SETS — collections of characters that a computer recognises from their binary representation, used to convert characters to binary code and vice versa.

Button pressed on keyboard → Binary signal sent to computer → Computer translates code using character set

Two Important Character Sets

1 ASCII

- Each character is given a 7-bit binary code — so ASCII can represent 128 different characters.
- An extra bit (0) may be added to the start of each binary code so each character uses 1 byte.
- The codes for numbers and letters are ordered (A comes before B comes before C...).

Character	Binary	Decimal
A	100 0001	65
B	100 0010	66
C	100 0011	67
a	110 0001	97
b	110 0010	98
c	110 0011	99

2 UNICODE®

- Covers all major languages, including ones that use different characters, like Greek, Russian and Chinese.
- Uses multiple bytes for each character.
- The first 128 characters in Unicode® are the same as ASCII.

The codes for capital letters, lowercase letters and digits are in ordered groups. So you can work out the code for one character given the code of another.

EXAMPLE

The ASCII code for 'g' is 103 in decimal.
Work out the Unicode® code for 'j'.

The codes for lowercase letters are ordered, so count up:

g	h	i	j
103	104	105	106

The ASCII code for 'j' is 106 in decimal.

So the Unicode® code for 'j' is 106 (in decimal), because the first 128 characters in Unicode® and ASCII are the same.

Storing Images

Representing Images

BITMAP — a type of image made up of pixels.

PIXEL — short for 'picture element', a tiny dot in a bitmap image. The colour of a pixel is stored using a binary code.

IMAGE SIZE — the number of pixels in a bitmap image. Often given as 'width × height'.

Computer screens can display millions of pixels.

Y'arr, I found me bits!

Colour Depth

COLOUR DEPTH — the number of bits used to represent each pixel.

The number of colours that can be used for a given colour depth follows this formula:

Total number of colours = 2^n (where n = colour depth)

E.g.   1-bit image: 2^1 = 2 colours (black and white)   4-bit image: 2^4 = 16 colours

Most devices use 24-bit colour depth, which can display over 16 million colours.

EXAMPLE

Convert this 2-bit image into binary.

Assign each colour a 2-bit code:
OO → white   O1 → light grey
1O → dark grey   11 → black

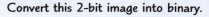

11	01	10	00
01	10	00	10
10	00	10	01
00	10	01	11

Image File Sizes

Use this formula to calculate file size:

File size (in bits)
= image size × colour depth
= width × height × colour depth

Increasing the image size or colour depth will usually give a higher quality image, but a larger file size.

EXAMPLE

Calculate the size in kB of a 100 × 100 pixel image with a colour depth of 16 bits.

File size = 100 × 100 × 16
        = 160 000 bits

160 000 bits
= 160 000 ÷ 8 = 20 000 bytes
= 20 000 ÷ 1000 = 20 kB

Storing Sound

Key Definitions

SAMPLING	Converting an analogue sound wave into digital data that can be read and stored by a computer.
SAMPLE RATE (SAMPLING FREQUENCY)	The number of samples taken per second. Usually measured in hertz (Hz) — 1 Hz = 1 sample per second.
SAMPLE RESOLUTION	The number of bits available for each sample.

Sound Sampling Process

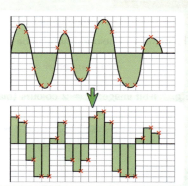

1. The amplitude of the sound wave is measured at fixed intervals, based on the sample rate. The measurements are only able to take certain values, based on the sample resolution.

2. The sound is recreated digitally based on the measurements taken. It will be a similar shape to the analogue wave, but will have lost some accuracy.

Sound File Sizes

File size (in bits) = Sample rate (in Hz) × sample resolution × length (in seconds)

A higher sample rate or sample resolution will give a higher quality sound file, but will increase the file size.

Couldn't agree more...

EXAMPLE

Calculate the file size in MB of a 50 second audio recording with a sample rate of 40 kHz and a sample resolution of 8 bits.

1 kHz = 1000 Hz	40 kHz = 40 000 Hz
Use the formula.	File size = 40 000 × 8 × 50 = 16 000 000 bits
Convert from bits to MB.	16 000 000 bits = 2 000 000 bytes
	= 2000 kB = 2 MB

RLE and Huffman Coding

Using RLE Compression

RUN — consecutive repeating data in a file.

RUN-LENGTH ENCODING (RLE) — lossless compression technique that looks for runs in a file. It is best used on data with lots of runs.

 Count the number of times the same data is repeated in a run.

 Store as data pairs, e.g. (length of run, data).

EXAMPLE

Explain how to use run-length encoding to compress the string 'Illooooonnnngggg'.

In 7-bit ASCII, this string is 112 bits.

1 Look for runs:
- 'l' × 3
- 'o' × 5
- 'n' × 4
- 'g' × 4

RLE can also be used on bitmap images and long runs of binary data.

2 4 data pairs to store:
(3, l) (5, o) (4, n) (4, g)

If each number uses 8 bits, then each data pair needs 15 bits. So RLE compresses the string to 60 bits.

Huffman Coding

HUFFMAN CODING — lossless compression technique. Data values in a file get a unique binary code with more frequent ones getting shorter codes.

Huffman codes are found using an algorithm.

Codes are shown in a table or a Huffman tree.

Encode or decode data with the table or tree.

m i s s i s s i p p i
1 × 'm', 4 × 'i',
4 × 's', 2 × 'p'

'i' and 's' are more frequent, so have shorter codes.

EXAMPLE

Use the Huffman tree to encode 'mississippi'.

Follow every path down the tree to find each code:

Character	'm'	'i'	's'	'p'
Huffman code	100	11	0	101

m i s s i s s i p p i
100 11 0 0 11 0 0 11 101 101 11

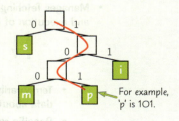

For example, 'p' is 101.

Calculating Bits Saved

Encoding data reduces the number of bits needed.

Uncompressed text often uses ASCII, which needs 7 bits per character.

Bits saved = bits needed for original data − bits needed for encoded data

Computer Systems and the CPU

Computer Systems

HARDWARE — the physical stuff in a computer system, e.g. keyboard, CPU, etc.

SOFTWARE — the programs that a computer system runs, such as application software (e.g. games, web browser) or system software (e.g. operating system).

EMBEDDED SYSTEMS — computers built into other devices, usually as control systems. E.g. they could control:

External pieces of hardware, e.g. a mouse, are called peripherals.

Dishwashers

Microwaves

Smartwatches

They're usually **easier** to design, **cheaper** to produce, and more **efficient** at their task than general purpose systems.

Non-embedded systems are things like laptops and smartphones.

Von Neumann Architecture

 CENTRAL PROCESSING UNIT (CPU) — where a computer processes all data and instructions.

In the **Von Neumann** architecture, data and instructions are both stored in the same memory.

 **Output Device**

Central Processing Unit (CPU)

Control Unit (CU)
- Controls the flow of data in and out of the CPU.
- Manages fetching, decoding and execution of instructions.

Arithmetic Logic Unit
- Does simple calculations.
- Performs binary shifts and logic operations.

Registers
- Temporarily hold small amounts of data about to be used by the CPU.
- Specific registers hold data for specific tasks.
- Faster to read/write to than other forms of memory.

Arrows show the flow of data (through buses).

 **Input Device**

 Memory — holds program instructions and data.

More About the CPU

Other Parts of the CPU

Buses

- Collections of wires.
- Transmit data between components of the CPU.

Clock

- Sends out a signal that cycles between 1 and 0.
- The signal helps to synchronise when to execute instructions.

Cache

- Stores regularly used data that can be accessed quickly.
- Very fast memory (slower than registers, faster than RAM).

Three Factors Affecting CPU Performance

1 **Number of cores** — each core processes data independently, so more cores means more instructions can be carried out per second.
Some software is designed to take advantage of multicore processing.

2 **Clock speed** — the number of instructions a single processor core can carry out per second.

3 **Cache size** — a larger cache gives the CPU faster access to more data.
Cache speed is also based on distance from the CPU.

Generally, CPUs with more cores, higher clock speeds and larger caches will have better performance, but cost more.

How do you pay for a new PC?
With cache.

Fetch-Execute Cycle

CPUs follow the **fetch-execute cycle**.
It repeats continuously while the computer is running.

1 **FETCH**
- The CU reads memory address of the next CPU instruction.
- Instruction copied from memory to one of the registers.
- Memory address is incremented to point to the next instruction.

2 **DECODE**
- The copied instruction is decoded by the CU.
- CU prepares for next step, e.g. by loading values into registers.

3 **EXECUTE**
Decoded instruction carried out. Examples of instructions:
- Load data from memory.
- Write data to memory.
- Do calculation or logic operation (using the **ALU**).

Section Five — Computer Systems and Databases

Memory

Memory and Storage

VOLATILE — power is required for the component to retain data.

NON-VOLATILE — the component retains data even when the power is turned off.

PRIMARY STORAGE — memory that is directly accessible by the CPU, e.g. RAM, ROM.

SECONDARY STORAGE — non-volatile storage not directly accessible by the CPU. Applications, user files and the OS are stored here when not in use.

Random Access Memory (RAM)

RAM — the main temporary memory in a computer.

 Volatile memory.

 Can be read from and written to.

 Programs and files are copied here from secondary storage while in use.

 Slower than the CPU cache, but faster than secondary storage.

More RAM usually means more apps and programs can be run smoothly at once.

I'm gonna RAM that stick u—

Jason!

Read Only Memory (ROM)

ROM — the main permanent memory in a computer.

 Non-volatile memory.

 Can only be read from, not written to.

 Small amount of memory built into the motherboard.

 Contains **BIOS** (Basic Input Output System) — instructions needed for the computer to boot up.

ROM is read only, but it is possible to update the BIOS on a ROM chip.

RAM/ROM Requirements

RAM/ROM needed depends on the system — typically...

NON-EMBEDDED SYSTEMS

- Have more RAM than ROM as writing data is common.
- ROM only used for BIOS.
- RAM and ROM are stored on the motherboard away from the CPU.

EMBEDDED SYSTEMS

- Have more ROM than RAM, as writing data isn't common.
- ROM stores all programs.
- RAM/ROM are stored on the same chip as the CPU.

Secondary Storage

Two Types of Internal Storage

1 Hard Disk Drives (HDDs)

- Moving parts.
- Store data magnetically on metal disks.
- Can be noisy.

2 Solid State Drives (SSDs)

- No moving parts.
- Store data in electrical circuits (flash storage).
- Usually quiet/silent.

Four Types of External Storage

1 Flash drives & memory cards — solid state storage, often to expand capacity of small devices.

2 Optical discs — e.g. CDs. Can be read-only, write-once or rewritable.

3 Magnetic tape — used to back up huge amounts of data.

4 External HDDs/SSDs — portable versions of internal storage.

Comparing Storage Types

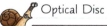 Optical Disc   Magnetic Tape   HDD   Memory Card   SSD
→ Average Read/Write Speed →

Optical Disc   Memory Card   SSD   HDD   Magnetic Tape
→ Average Capacity →

 Magnetic Tape   Optical Disc   HDD   Memory Card   SSD
→ Average Cost (per GB) →

- Solid state storage is shock resistant... but has limited rewrites.
- Magnetic storage has a long read/write life... but is easily damaged by impacts.

Cloud Storage

Usually an HDD or SSD.

CLOUD STORAGE — online service where files are uploaded to a remote server.

Pros of the cloud	Cons of the cloud
Access files from any device.	Requires Internet connection.
Easy to increase storage space.	Stored data can be vulnerable to hackers.
No need for expensive hardware and the staff to manage it.	Unclear who has ownership of data.
Host provides security and backups.	Relies on host for security and backups.
Automatic updates.	Expensive subscription fees.

System Software — The OS

I think you've got the wrong driver...

Function	Features
1 **I/O device management and drivers**	• Communicates with I/O (input/output) devices connected to the system, using drivers. • Chooses correct drivers for connected hardware on startup. • Installs drivers for new hardware and updates drivers automatically.
2 **Providing a platform for applications**	GUI = Graphical User Interface • Allows applications to run and grants them access to hardware and I/O devices as needed. • User interfaces allow users to interact with a computer — GUIs are designed for everyday users. • Desktops often have windows, icons, menus and pointers, while smartphones with touchscreens allow users to tap, pinch and swipe.
3 **Memory management**	• Moves application data to main memory when in use and removes it when it's no longer needed. • Allocates memory addresses so apps don't overwrite or interfere with each other.
4 **Processor management**	To multitask, the CPU swaps between processes rapidly. • Carries out processes, one at a time. • Prioritises tasks using scheduling — high-priority processes are executed first, while other processes wait in a queue.
5 **File and disk management**	• Organises files into a hierarchical structure of folders. • Deals with the naming, saving, moving, editing and deleting of files and folders. • Splits the hard disk into sectors and decides where files are written to. • Maintains the hard disk with utility software. The OS uses extensions to match files with apps.
6 **System security**	• Controls which users are granted or denied access to the computer system. • Grants users access to specific data — e.g. their own personal account, but not that of other users. • Uses anti-theft measures to prevent access for other users — e.g. password or PIN protection.

System Software — Utilities

Defragmentation Software

UTILITY PROGRAMS — software designed to help maintain a computer system.

Defragmentation software reorganises an HDD by putting related data back together. This speeds up reading/writing files as the read/write head no longer has to move as much.

> SSDs don't need to be defragmented — they can access fragmented files quickly.

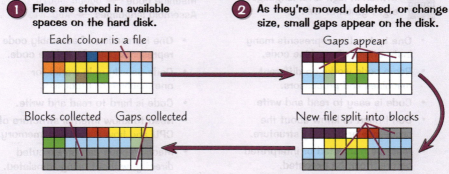

1 Files are stored in available spaces on the hard disk.

Each colour is a file

2 As they're moved, deleted, or change size, small gaps appear on the disk.

Gaps appear

Blocks collected Gaps collected

New file split into blocks

4 Defragmentation puts the fragmented files back together. It also groups any free space.

3 When writing new files to the disk, the OS splits them into smaller blocks to fill the gaps.

Six More Utilities

1 **Compression software** — reduces size of files by permanently or temporarily removing data from them.

2 **Disk health utility** — scans the hard drive and aims to fix issues such as corrupted data.

3 **Encryption software** — scrambles (encrypts) data to stop third parties from accessing it.
> To decrypt it back to its original form, a special 'key' is needed.

4 **Backup utility** — allows scheduled backups of files and settings. These are stored externally and can be restored when data is lost.

5 **Virus scanner** — inspects files, checking for viruses. The list of known viruses should be updated regularly.

6 **System cleanup utility** — removes temporary files left behind by programs like web browsers.

Languages and Translators

High-Level Languages

HIGH-LEVEL LANGUAGE — a programming language that is easy for humans to understand.

The majority of code is written in high-level languages, e.g. Python or C#.

- One instruction represents many instructions of machine code.
- Same code works on different machines and processors.
- Code is easy to read and write.
- Don't need to know about the processor or memory structure.
- Must be translated or interpreted before it can be executed.
- Slower and less memory efficient.

Low-Level Languages

LOW-LEVEL LANGUAGE — a programming language close to what a CPU would actually do.

Often used for embedded systems.

Machine code ➤ 00000 00010 00011...
Assembly languages ➤ ADD r4, r2...

- One instruction of assembly code represents one of machine code.
- Code usually only works for one machine or processor.
- Code is hard to read and write.
- Need to know internal structure of CPU and how it manages memory.
- Machine code can be executed directly, without being translated.
- Faster and more memory efficient.

Three Types of Translator

TRANSLATOR — a program that allows source code to be understood and executed by a computer.

1 COMPILER

- Translates high-level code into machine code, all at the same time.
- Only needs to be used once, creating an executable file.
- Returns a list of errors for whole program when compiling is complete.
- Compiling can take a long time, but program runs quickly once compiled.

2 INTERPRETER

- Translates and runs high-level code, one instruction at a time, using its own machine code subroutines.
- Used every time code is run.
- Stops and returns first error found.
- Programs run more slowly.

3 ASSEMBLER

- Translates assembly language into machine code.
- Each CPU uses a specific assembly language, and each assembly language has its own unique assembler.

Relational Databases and SQL

Relational Databases

DATABASE — data collected in tables (columns = fields, rows = records).

PRIMARY KEY — a field which uniquely identifies a record.

FOREIGN KEY — a field which references a primary key of another table.

Relational databases have multiple tables, linked with primary and foreign keys:

ID is the primary key.

Each field has a data type, e.g. integer.

Table: merchList

ID	item	price
1	Cap	£12
2	Mug	£5
3	Fleece	£30

Table: orders

orderNo	ID	shipTo
OO1	3	Chester
OO2	3	Glasgow
OO3	1	Penzance

orderNo is the primary key.

ID is a foreign key, linking to merchList table.

Data is stored in one place and referenced, which reduces inconsistencies and saves storage space. For security, specific users can have access restricted to certain tables.

Searching Data with SQL

SQL is used to create, search and maintain database tables.

Table: cars

ID	regNum	year	fuel
1	JZ18 IQZ	2018	Petrol
2	XJ23 QSI	2023	Diesel
3	IQ21 UIK	2021	Petrol

SELECT and **FROM** specify which fields to return.

Use * to return all fields...

```
SELECT * FROM cars
```

...or list which field(s) to return from each record.

```
SELECT ID FROM cars
```

WHERE filters records using a condition. **ORDER BY** sorts the results.

Use AND or OR to check multiple conditions.

```
SELECT regNum, year FROM cars
WHERE year < 2020 OR fuel != "Diesel"
ORDER BY year DESC
```

regNum	year
IQ21 UIK	2021
JZ18 IQZ	2018

ASC sorts in ascending order. DESC sorts in descending order.

Changing Data with SQL

DELETE — to delete records.

```
DELETE FROM cars
WHERE fuel = "Diesel"
```

Use conditions to determine what data to change or delete.

UPDATE & SET — to edit records.

```
UPDATE cars SET year = 2022 WHERE ID = 2
```

INSERT INTO & VALUES — to add records.

```
INSERT INTO cars (ID, year) VALUES (4, 2020)
```

Only specify fields when adding incomplete records.

Section Five — Computer Systems and Databases

Types of Network

Network Hardware

NETWORK — a connected group of devices that share data and resources.

Switch — connects devices on a LAN.

Router — transmits data between different networks.

Network Interface Card (NIC) — lets a device connect to a network.

Wireless Access Point (WAP) — lets a device connect wirelessly.

LANs — Local Area Networks

LANs cover small geographical areas on one site — e.g. businesses or schools.

LAN hardware is usually owned by the organisation using it.

Typical devices on a LAN

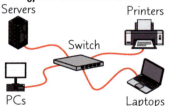

Servers   Printers   Switch   PCs   Laptops

WANs — Wide Area Networks

WANs connect LANs in different geographical locations.

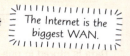
The Internet is the biggest WAN.

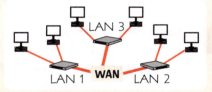

LAN 3   LAN 1   **WAN**   LAN 2

Organisations hire infrastructure from a company who own and manage the **WAN**.

More expensive to set up than LANs.

PANs — Personal Area Networks

PANs connect devices over short ranges — e.g. mobile devices in one room.

PANs often use Bluetooth®. It has a strong signal but a short range.

Ideal for single users on the move as no extra hardware needed.

Pros and Cons of Networking

PROS	CONS
• Users can access the same files.	• Can be expensive to set up.
• Hardware is shared between devices.	• Vulnerable to hacking, and malware can easily spread across the network.
• Simultaneous software updates.	• Disruptive to users if servers fail.
• Easy communication between users.	• Large networks need maintaining.
• Users can log in from any device.	

Networks and Topologies

Wired Networks

BANDWIDTH — the amount of data that can be sent over a network in a given time.

Wired networks use cables to connect devices — there are different types of cable:

Coaxial — a single copper wire surrounded by plastic insulation and metallic mesh to shield from outside interference.

 Fibre optic — transmits data as light. Can send data over long distances with little interference.

Low cost
Low bandwidth

 CAT 5e/CAT 6 — copper wires twisted together in pairs to reduce internal interference. Used in homes and offices.

High cost
High bandwidth

Wireless Networks

Radio waves transmit data between devices on wireless networks.

⊕ Convenient to use on the move.
⊕ Cheaper than wired networks.
⊕ Easy to add more users.

⊖ Less secure than wired networks.
⊖ Usually have a lower bandwidth.
⊖ Signal strength affected by distance, interference and physical obstructions.

Star Topology

All devices connect to a central switch or server that controls the network.

Star Topology

PROS
- Network unaffected if a device fails.
- Easy to add more devices.
- High performance.
- Very few data collisions.

CONS
- Expensive for wired networks.
- Switch is a single point of failure.
- Switch limits number of devices.

Bus Topology

One backbone cable (called the bus) connects all devices.

Bus Topology
Terminators stop data reflecting.

PROS
- Network unaffected if a device fails.
- Not dependent on a central switch.
- Relatively cheap to set up.

CONS
- Data collisions are common.
- Not suitable for large networks.
- Stops working if bus cable breaks.

Network Protocols

Network Layers

NETWORK PROTOCOL — rules for how devices communicate and how data is sent across a network.

LAYER — a group of protocols with similar functions.

> Each layer is self-contained and data can only be passed between adjacent layers.

TCP/IP Model

Layer	Name	Function
4	Application Layer	Providing networking services to applications.
3	Transport Layer	Splitting data into equal-sized packets and making sure they're sent from and delivered to the correct devices.
2	Internet Layer	Addressing packets and directing them over a network.
1	Link Layer	Physically sending data over cables and hardware.

4. Application Layer Protocols

 Hyper Text Transfer Protocol (HTTP) — web browsers use it to access websites and web servers.

 HTTP Secure (HTTPS) — encrypts website information sent and received for security.

 File Transfer Protocol (FTP) — accesses, edits and moves files between devices on a network.

 Simple Mail Transfer Protocol (SMTP) — sends and transfers emails between servers.

 Instant Messaging Access Protocol (IMAP) — retrieves emails from a server.

3. Transport Layer Protocols

Transmission Control Protocol (TCP) — splits and reassembles data packets so they're read in order. Checks packets have been received and resends if they haven't.

Reliable, good for downloading files.

User Datagram Protocol (UDP) — splits data into packets that may be received and read out of order. Only sends each packet once and doesn't check they've been received.

Fast, efficient, good for streaming.

2. Internet Layer Protocols

 Internet Protocol (IP) — unique numbers called **IP addresses** identify and direct packets between devices and routers (packet switching). Packets change routes based on network traffic.

1. Link Layer Protocols

 These are **families** of protocols that work on the same layer.

Wi-Fi® — used in wireless LANs (WLANs). Data is sent in frames (not packets) over a range of frequency bands and channels.

Ethernet — used in wired LANs.

Network Security Threats

Three Forms of Malware

MALWARE — software designed to damage, disrupt or gain illegal access to a network. Often installed onto a device without the owner's knowledge or consent. E.g. as an email attachment or hidden on removable media.

1. **Viruses** — attached to other files. Run and replicate when the file is opened.

2. **Trojans** — malware disguised as legitimate software. Don't self-replicate.

3. **Spyware** — monitors user actions like key presses and sends info to the hacker.

Three Types of Social Engineering

SOCIAL ENGINEERING — manipulating people to gain sensitive information or illegal access to a network.

1. **Phishing** — criminals send emails or texts posing as a real business. They may contain links to fake websites that ask users to update their personal information, which the criminals steal.
   Messages often have typos. Can be spotted by anti-phishing filters.

2. **Shouldering** — watching a person's activity, typically over their shoulder, in order to steal their private information. E.g. spying someone's PIN at an ATM.
   Can be avoided by being discreet.

3. **Blagging** — making up a story or pretending to be someone else to persuade the victim to share information or do something unusual. Often involves pressuring them to act before they've had time to think.
   Biometric data can't be 'blagged'.

Pharming

You have 131 viruses, Dave.

PHARMING — an attack where users are redirected to a fake website that looks just like the real one.

- Malware can automatically send users from real sites to fake ones.
- E.g. fake banking or shopping sites trick users into inputting personal information like bank details.
- Risks reduced by using web filters and anti-malware software.

Two Types of Penetration Testing

Organisations hire specialists to simulate attacks — they identify and report weaknesses in a network's security. The weaknesses can be fixed to help to protect against real network attacks.

1. Simulates a **malicious insider**. The tester is given user credentials for a system to see what they can do with them.

2. Simulates an **external attack**. The tester tries to hack into the system from the outside.

Network Security Measures

Six Ways to Defend Networks

CYBER SECURITY — protecting networks, programs, computers and data from damage, cyber attacks and unauthorised access.

I've made it through the third firewall.

Hurry up Doris — they're almost onto us.

1 **Encryption** — data is translated into a code that needs a specific key to access. Essential for sending data over a network securely.

> Encrypted data is called cipher text.
> Unencrypted data is called plain text.

2 **Anti-Malware Software** — prevents malware from damaging a network and the devices on it.

3 **MAC Address Filtering** — blocks devices from accessing a network unless their unique MAC address is known and trusted.

4 **Firewall** — software or hardware that examines all data entering and leaving a network. Identifies threats using a set of security rules to block unwanted data.

5 **User Access Levels** — control which parts of the network different groups of users can access. Limits who can access sensitive data.

6 **Automatic Software Updates** — used to patch known security holes in a piece of software.

Four Types of Authentication

USER AUTHENTICATION — confirming the identity of a user trying to access a network.

1 **Passwords** — should be strong (long with a mix of letters, numbers and symbols) and changed regularly. Weak or default passwords are a big security risk.

 `bossman` ✗ Weak

 `B9£l@sTr!y*A` ✓ Strong

2 **Biometric Measures** — identify people by scanning a unique body part, e.g. fingerprint, retina, etc. to prevent unauthorised access.

3 **Email Confirmation** — used by web services that require account registration to confirm an email address belongs to the person registering.

4 **CAPTCHA** — a simple task, like clicking images containing a certain object. Designed to prevent programs from automatically doing things like creating user accounts on a website.

Technology and the Digital Divide

Five Important Areas of Technology

1 Mobile Technologies
Smartphones help people stay in touch easily, but also let them neglect face-to-face interaction.

2 Wearable Technologies
Devices can promote safety and healthy lifestyles, but can also infringe on privacy.

3 Computer-Based Implants
Can provide great health benefits, but may be expensive and lead to less privacy.

4 Autonomous Vehicles
Can be safer than normal vehicles, but may not be able to deal with unpredictable situations as well as a human could.

5 Cloud Storage
Can provide a convenient service and have environmental benefits, but may also be more vulnerable to hackers.

The Internet and Business

Impacts of the Internet

- People shop and bank over the Internet, so these websites need to have good cyber security.
- Places that offer (free) Wi-Fi® have an obligation to protect users, especially children.
- Digital purchases and subscriptions create issues over ownership, and access can be lost.

Impacts on Business

- Jobs can be applied for online, but this can make it harder for people who don't have Internet access.
- Smartphones make it easy for work to intrude into other areas of life. This can be stressful for employees.
- Pop-up ads can make a free service profitable for a company, but users can feel swamped by them.

Three Causes of the Digital Divide

DIGITAL DIVIDE — the inequality caused by unequal access to technology.

1 Devices and an Internet connection can be too expensive.

2 Urban areas often have greater network coverage than rural areas.

3 People may have difficulty adopting new technology — usually due to not being taught how to use it or not growing up with it.

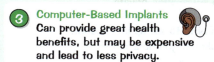

There is a global divide due to different access to technology in different countries. Projects and charities have been set up to combat the digital and global divide.

Ethical Issues

Anonymity

Online anonymity lets people be open and honest whilst protecting their identity.

Being anonymous online can also cause issues, particularly on social media:

1 **CYBERBULLYING** — using digital technology to deliberately intimidate, insult or humiliate someone online.

2 **TROLLING** — making comments online to deliberately provoke an argument.

Privacy

People generally want to keep their personal information private, but this can be hard to do on the Internet.

- Websites may ask for a name and date of birth to set up an account.
- Social media encourages users to share photos, job details, etc.
- Cloud services store personal files on their servers.

Privacy agreements say what a company can do with your information. You have to accept before using their service.

Privacy settings can sometimes be changed to make data more private. They're often fairly relaxed by default.

Users must trust companies to keep their data secure from leaks or theft. Some privacy agreements allow your personal data to be sold to other companies.

Censorship and Surveillance

CENSORSHIP — controlling what information people can access.

Three things countries and governments may restrict access to:

CENSORED

1 Illegal content or websites supporting criminal acts like drug use or hate speech.

2 Age-restricted content like gambling or pornography.

3 Foreign websites or websites that are critical of the government.

SURVEILLANCE — monitoring what people are accessing on the Internet.

- Government intelligence agencies look for words or phrases related to illegal activities, e.g. terrorism.
- Internet Service Providers may keep records of websites visited by customers.

Programs like packet sniffers can monitor Internet traffic.

18+ Parents and schools also use parental-control software to filter content and monitor activity.

Legal Issues

Six Data Protection Principles

When an organisation stores someone's personal data on their system, that person is entitled to certain rights, summarised by these principles:

1. Data must be used in a fair, lawful and transparent way.

2. Data must be used for the specified purposes.

3. Data gathered should be relevant and not excessive.

4. Data must be accurate and kept up to date.

5. Data should not be kept longer than necessary.

6. Data should be kept safe and secure.

This means they have a legal obligation to have good cyber security.

Organisations must register with the government before collecting personal data.

Cyber Crime

CYBER CRIME — any illegal activity that involves computers.

HACKING — gaining access to a system by exploiting weaknesses.

Hackers might:
• steal or ransom data
• damage or destroy data
• infect networks with malware

Companies can employ 'good hackers' to perform penetration testing.

Computer Misuse Act

Introduced three new offences to stop hacking and cyber crime.

1. Gaining unauthorised access to a private network or device.

2. Gaining unauthorised access in order to commit a crime.

3. Unauthorised modification of computer material.

It also makes it illegal to make, supply or obtain malware.

The original act of computer misuse.

Four Types of Network Attack

Hackers use lots of different methods to attack systems:

Attack	How it works
1. Passive	Data on a network is intercepted using monitoring hardware or software like packet sniffers.
2. Active	Malware or other means are used to attack a system directly.
3. Brute force	Automated software is used to try millions of potential passwords until one works.
4. Denial of service (DoS)	Hacker prevents users from accessing a network or website by flooding it with useless traffic/requests.

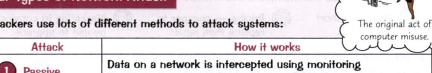

Environmental Issues

Natural Resources

Electronic devices contain lots of raw materials.

 Crude oil is used to make plastics for packaging, casing and other parts.

 Precious metals are used in wiring and circuit boards. E.g. gold, silver, copper, mercury, palladium, platinum and indium.

Non-renewable resources like coal, oil and gas are used to generate electricity.

Extracting these materials uses lots of energy, creates pollution (e.g. greenhouse gases) and depletes scarce resources.

Electricity Usage

Devices use a lot of energy in the form of electricity.

Computers and servers also generate heat. They are often cooled using fans or air-conditioned rooms, which uses even more electricity.

There are ways to reduce electricity waste:

Problem	Solution
Desktops, laptops and smartphones are left idle.	Sleep and hibernate modes reduce power consumption.
Servers don't use all of their processing power.	Multiple virtual servers can run on one physical server.

Is all this necessary?

Probably.

E-Waste

Millions of electronic devices are discarded every year.

Three ways device manufacturers and retailers can contribute to this problem:

1. Providing short warranties.
2. Pricing — cheaper to replace than repair.
3. Marketing to convince people to upgrade.

To cut costs, lots of e-waste is sent to countries where regulations are less strict. Most ends up in landfill and can be a hazard — toxic chemicals can leak into groundwater and harm wildlife.

 The Waste Electric and Electronic Equipment (WEEE) directive covers:
- Disposing of e-waste safely.
- Promoting reuse, e.g. refurbishing broken devices.
- Recycling materials, e.g. extracting precious metals.

COAN041